Cattle

Kathleen Reitmann

www.av2books.com

Step 1
Go to **www.av2books.com**

Step 2
Enter this unique code
HDQGUAMW8

Step 3
Explore your interactive eBook!

AV2

FARM ANIMALS

Cattle

Start!

AV2 is optimized for use on any device

Your interactive eBook comes with...

Audio
Listen to the entire book read aloud

Videos
Watch informative video clips

Weblinks
Gain additional information for research

Try This!
Complete activities and hands-on experiments

Key Words
Study vocabulary, and complete a matching word activity

Quizzes
Test your knowledge

Slideshows
View images and captions

View new titles and product videos at www.av2books.com

Cattle

Contents

Ca

Cattle are large animals that live on a farm.

Farmers raise cattle for food, milk, and leather.

ttle

More cattle live in Texas than in any other state.

Baby cattle are called calves.

Most calves are born in the spring.

A calf weighs about **65 pounds** at birth.

Female cattle that have at least one calf are called **cows**.

Male cattle are called **bulls**. Bulls are larger than cows.

Cattle have hoofs instead of feet.

Each hoof has two claws that protect cattle when they walk.

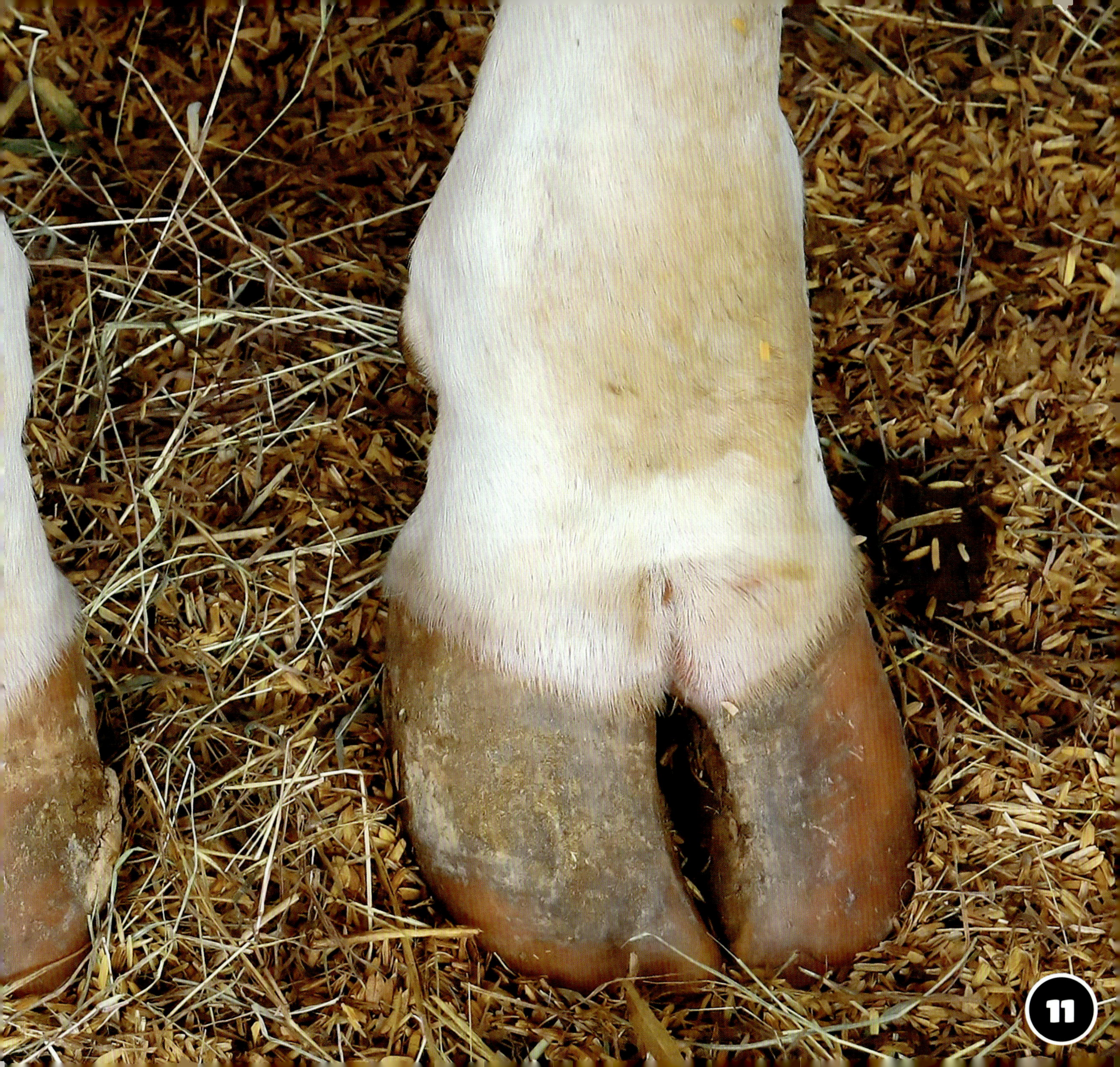

Cattle skins are called hides.

Hides can be used to make leather. People use leather for clothes, bags, and shoes.

The oldest known leather shoe is 5,500 years old.

Cattle talk to each other by mooing.

Each moo is unique, like a human voice.

Cattle eat grass and weeds.

Their stomachs have four parts. Each part stores food for later.

Cattle **do not have** top front teeth.

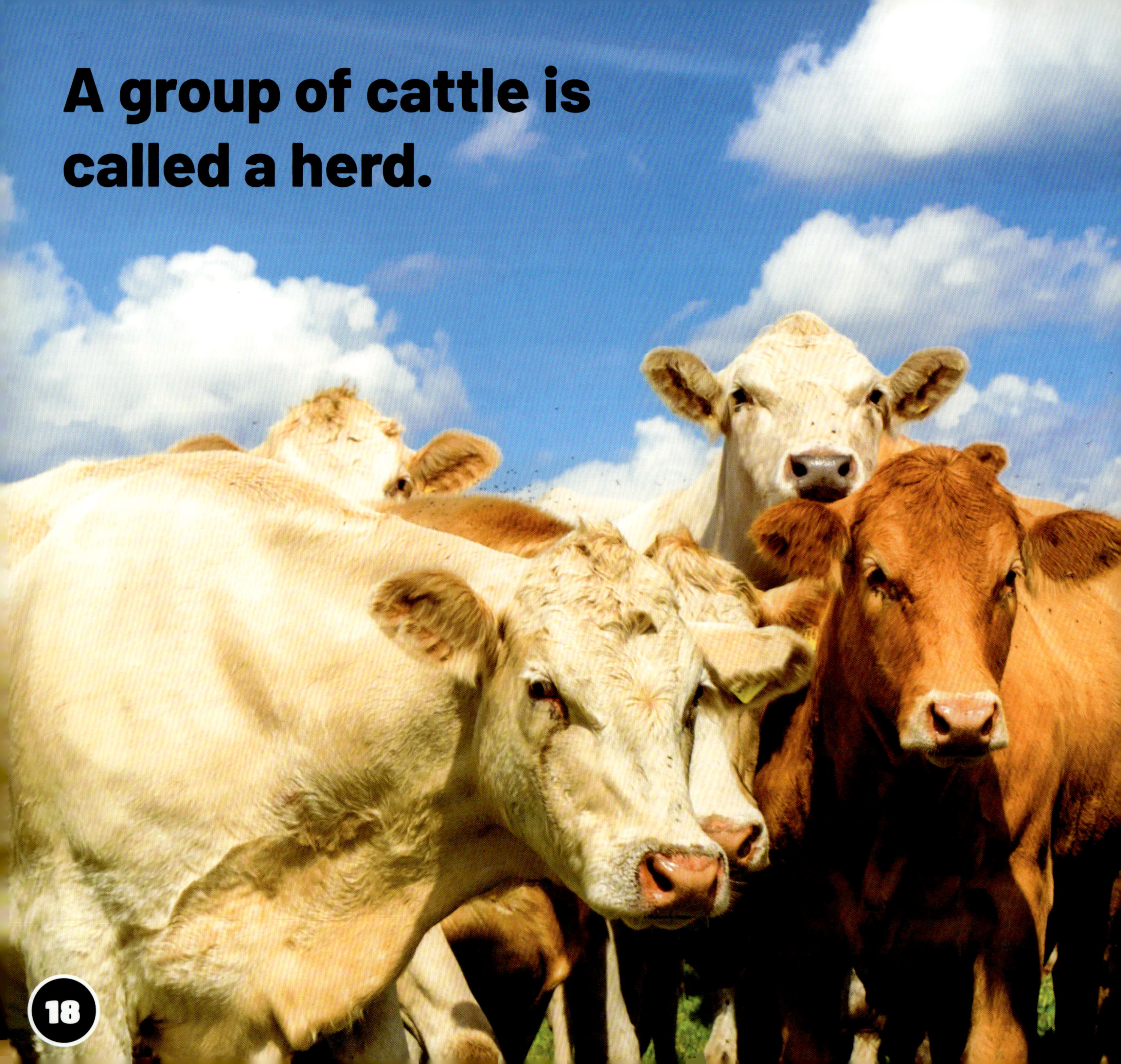

A group of cattle is called a herd.

Cattle herds travel together to keep safe.

Cattle eat large amounts of grass.

Farmers must provide cattle with an open space and grass to feed on.

CATTLE FACTS

These pages provide detailed information that expands on the interesting facts found in the book. They are intended to be used by adults as a learning support to help young readers round out their knowledge of each unique animal featured in the *Farm Animals* series and why it is kept and raised on farms.

Pages 4–5

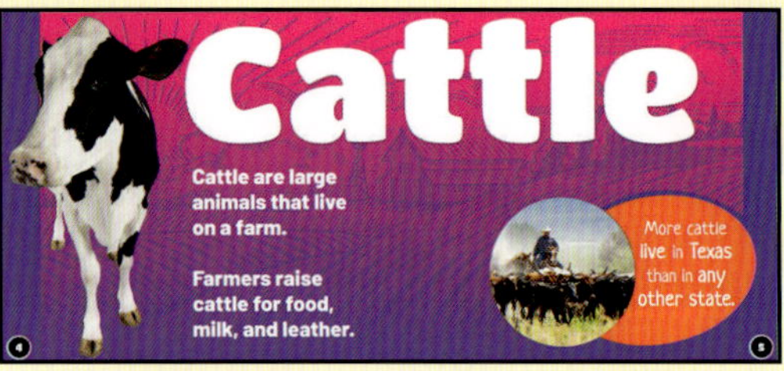

Cattle are large animals that live on a farm. There are about 29 million cattle in the United States. According to the United States Department of Agriculture, cattle are raised and sold in every state. However, 45 percent of cattle are raised in only five states. They are Texas, Nebraska, South Dakota, Kansas, and Oklahoma. Texas farms are home to about 4.3 million cattle.

Pages 6–7

Baby cattle are called calves. A cow usually has her first calf when she is about two years old. Most calves are born during a 90-day window in the spring. Calves are weaned when they are about six months old.

Pages 8–9

Female cattle that have at least one calf are called cows. Before a cow has a calf, she is called a heifer. Cows are the most common farm animals around the world. Male cattle that are used to mate with cows are called bulls. A cow can weigh up to 2,400 pounds (1,100 kilograms). A full-grown bull can weigh up to 4,000 pounds (1,814 kg).

Pages 10–11

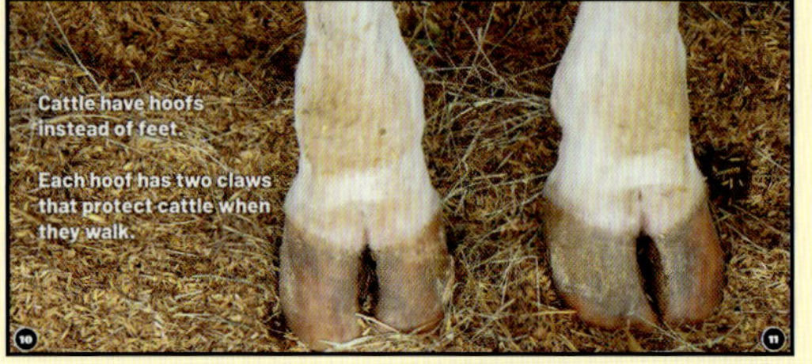

Cattle have hoofs instead of feet. Each hoof has two toes with a horn-covered claw. The horn covering is hard and protects the sensitive tissue underneath while cattle stand and walk. The claws on hoofs are like shock absorbers. They help even out the cattle's weight as they move. Healthy hoofs protect cattle from certain types of diseases and infections.

Pages 12–13

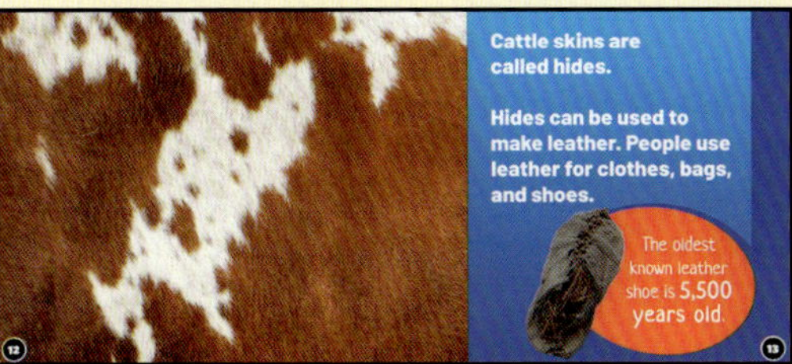

Cattle skins are called hides. People have been using cattle hides to make leather for more than 7,000 years. Hides are treated with chemicals to preserve them. This process is called tanning and was developed around 400 BC by the Egyptians and Hebrews. Leather is used to make everything from shoes and belts to footballs and furniture.

Pages 14–15

Cattle talk to each other by mooing. Scientists have discovered that each moo is unique. Each cow produces a specific call. When a cow is near her calf, she makes low moans, but when she cannot find her calf, she makes high-pitched calls. Calves call out to their mothers when they are hungry. Scientists can tell the age of a calf by the call it makes.

Pages 16–17

Cattle eat grass and weeds. They are well adapted for grazing because they have special teeth. Cattle have 32 teeth, but no top front teeth. Instead, they have a gummy pad to help tear apart grass. Cattle have stomachs with four compartments. Each compartment stores food that the cattle regurgitate and chew over and over. Stored food is called cud.

Pages 18–19

A group of cattle is called a herd. Cattle move in herds because it is difficult for a predator to catch them when they are grouped together. Being part of a herd provides camouflage. Colors and markings on cattle blend together, making it difficult to see where one animal ends and the next one begins. This helps to confuse predators.

Pages 20–21

Cattle eat large amounts of grass. Natural pasture grasses are the most important source of food for cattle. Eating hundreds of different grasses and bushes helps cattle attain all the nutrition they need to be healthy. About 60 percent of the world's farmland is used for grazing.

KEY WORDS

Research has shown that as much as 65 percent of all written material published in English is made up of 300 words. These 300 words cannot be taught using pictures or learned by sounding them out. They must be recognized by sight. This book contains 59 common sight words to help young readers improve their reading fluency and comprehension. This book also teaches young readers several important content words, such as proper nouns. These words are paired with pictures to aid in learning and improve understanding.

Page	Sight Words First Appearance
4	a, and, animals, are, farm, food, for, large, live, on, that
5	any, in, more, other, state, than
7	about, at, most, the
8	have, one
10	each, feet, has, of, they, two, use, walk, when
13	and, be, can, is, make, old, people, to, years
14	by, like, talk
17	do, eat, four, later, not, parts, their
18	group
19	keep, together
20	an, must, need, open, with

Page	Content Words First Appearance
4	cattle, farmers, leather, milk
5	Texas
7	birth, calves, pounds, spring
8	cows
9	bulls
10	claws, hoofs
13	bags, clothes, hide, skin, shoes
14	moo, voice
17	grass, stomachs, teeth, weeds
18	herd
20	amounts, space

Published by AV2
350 5th Avenue, 59th Floor New York, NY 10118
Website: www.av2books.com

Library of Congress Cataloging-in-Publication Data

Names: Reitmann, Kathleen, author.
Title: Cattle / Kathleen Reitmann
Description: New York, NY : AV2, [2019] | Series: Farm animals | Audience: Grades 2-3 |
Identifiers: LCCN 2019040187 (print) | LCCN 2019040188 (ebook) | ISBN 9781791116361 (library binding) | ISBN 9781791116378 (paperback) | ISBN 9781791116392 (ebook other) | ISBN 9781791116385 (ebook other)
Subjects: LCSH: Cattle--Juvenile literature. | Livestock--Juvenile literature. Classification: LCC SF197.5 .R45 2019 (print) | LCC SF197.5 (ebook) | DDC 636.2--dc23
LC record available at https://lccn.loc.gov/2019040187
LC ebook record available at https://lccn.loc.gov/2019040188

Printed in Guangzhou, China
1 2 3 4 5 6 7 8 9 0 24 23 22 21 20

022020
100919

Art Director: Terry Paulhus Project Coordinators: Sara Cucini and Ryan Smith

Every reasonable effort has been made to trace ownership and to obtain permission to reprint copyright material. The publisher would be pleased to have any errors or omissions brought to its attention so that they may be corrected in subsequent printings.

The publisher acknowledges Alamy, iStock, Getty Images, and Shutterstock as the primary image suppliers for this title.